Unmasking

The Quiet Strength in Vulnerable Moments

Samantha Crawford

BookLeaf Publishing

India | USA | UK

Made with ❤ on the BookLeaf Publishing Platform
www.bookleafpub.in
www.bookleafpub.com

Dedication

To my amazing wife and our beautiful son, whose love has been my guiding light, this chronicle of recovery and healing is for you.

Preface

Trigger Warning: This book contains content that may be triggering, including themes of mental illness, trauma, depression, anxiety, and suicidal thoughts. The poems reflect deeply personal experiences with these topics and may evoke strong emotional responses. Reader discretion is advised, and if you are struggling with similar issues, please consider seeking support from a mental health professional or a trusted person in your life.

This book of poetry is a record of my experiences while undergoing intensive treatment for mental illness. It covers a period when I faced many incredibly challenging symptoms, including but not limited to severe depression, anxiety, and chronic passive suicidality with periods of active suicidal thoughts. The poems included here were written during this challenging time and are organized chronologically, not thematically.

By presenting the poems in the order that they were written, I aim to reflect the reality of recovery—an uneven journey with ups and downs. This arrangement captures the true nature of my mental health experience, showing how progress can be non-linear and how emotions fluctuate over time.

I hope that this book offers insight and connection to those who may be navigating similar challenges. These poems are both a personal account and an attempt to provide a sense of solidarity for anyone facing their own battles with mental illness.

Acknowledgements

To my wife, whose unwavering support and understanding have been my guiding light through the darkest of times—thank you for your boundless love and encouragement.

To my son, whose innocent joy and laughter remind me daily of the beauty in small moments—your presence has been a source of immense strength.

To my therapist, whose expertise and unwavering support have saved my life—thank you for never giving up on me, and for keeping the hope alive for the future when I couldn't see it myself. Your guidance has been a true gift, and I'll always be grateful for the way you've shown me what safety, security, and trust feel like.

To my sister, whose strength and resilience is truly amazing—your dedication to your children, even in unbearably painful times, has profoundly impacted both their lives and mine. You have shown me what it means to be a parent—thank you for being a daily source of inspiration.

To my peers in group, whose shared experiences and

camaraderie have offered solace and inspiration—thank you for walking this path with me.

To my best friend, whose unconditional love and support across years, distance, and chapters has kept me going time and time again—I am so grateful to have you in my life.

To my wife's best friend and sister, whose unwavering support for her has been a source of comfort and strength for both of us—your kindness and love are invaluable.

To my dear friend, mentor, and confidant, whose understanding and nonjudgmental nature have meant the world to me—through all the ups and downs, I am deeply grateful that our bond remains strong.

I Am Not A Poet

1

I am not a poet
stringing together words
grasping beauty
creating eloquence
turning experiences
into art
holding myself up
on a pedestal of language
inflicting wounds with a creative power.

I am a poem
ready to be read
to be felt
to be heard.

I am a poem,
already with a life of my own.

Sterilized By Shame

In sterile rooms, the hours crawl,
white coats drift like ghosts,
the bed is hard, the light is harsh,
isolation grows.

Pills and whispers fill the air,
time ticks slow and cold,
with every glance and measured breath,
I feel less than human, controlled.

No privacy in this quiet void,
no autonomy to claim,
fear of being trapped inside
this cage of sterile shame.

In the silence, shadows loom,
hope seems out of reach,
a fragile dream that fades away,
in a world that's cold and bleak.

Gratitude's Light

Shadows deep, where sorrows weave,
a flicker of hope, I still believe.
Through storms of mind, in darkest night,
gratitude sparks a healing light.

Through the haze of pain and fear,
a single light, bright and near.
For every scar, a tale of might,
a journey back to morning light.

In every leaf and buzz of bees,
a comfort found among the trees.
For every storm, a flower's birth,
a strength drawn from Mother Earth.

A gentle breeze, a friend's kind word,
in gratitude, my heart is stirred.
Through the battle, fierce and long,
gratitude becomes my song.

A sunrise warm, a breath so free,
a simple joy that carries me.
Through the storm, I find my way,
I'm so grateful for another day.

Survival

In the quiet dark,
anxiety buzzes,
depression drags.

Two shadows
wrestle in my mind,
one screaming danger,
the other whispering
there's no escape.

Surviving is a win,
in a world where
peace feels
like a distant echo.

A Quiet Battle

I bear my burden in silence,
a heavy weight unseen,
to spare them from the grief
of wondering what could have been.

I quietly care for my wounds,
patching them up piece by piece
keeping them hidden from sight,
a quiet storm raging within.

I endure, breath by breath,
taming my darkest thoughts,
to ensure they never doubt
their immense worthiness.

A Letter To My Therapist

In the quiet space between your words and mine,
I find a sanctuary where my truth can shine.
Through the years of work, together we have tread,
untangling the threads of all that I have said.

You hold my pain with a strong hand,
creating a safe space where I can finally stand.
But still I feel the weight of all that is left undone,
a journey yet to finish, a fight yet to be won.

Depression's shadow lingers near,
and suicidality whispers words that I fear.
But in your presence, I find a light,
guiding me through my darkest night.

Your honesty sharp but never unkind,
helps me confront the bales in my mind.
You see me fully, with all of my flaws and fears,
allowing space for my lows, through the years.

In your eyes, there's no judgment, only grace,
a reflection of trust in this sacred space.
Your bluntness cuts through my persistent shame,
challenging me to see the same.

There is still so much work left on this road,
but thanks to you, I carry a lighter load.
Together we face the storms that brew,
with each step forward, I learn something new.

So thank you for walking this road by my side,
and being my life jacket through each rising tide.
With your support, I'll continue to face my inner fray,
and find the courage to keep trying, day after day.

7. Beyond The Mirror

Looking inward,
I see her hiding away.

Facing an empty page,
Pen in hand, afraid to stay.

Seeing childhood through innocent eyes,
My healing is underway.

A glimpse of her heart
Overwhelms me with dismay.

A view of life through a fractured lens—
In the mirror, I feel her pain.

Afraid I won't be able to look away,
Afraid of what may happen if I stay.

The Distance We Face

In your presence, I found refuge,
a place where my fears could dissolve.
Your words held warmth, your heart, an open space,
a haven for the heaviness I carried.
Now, I am adrift in a storm of my own making,
A squall that distorts and overwhelms.
Letting you go feels like a deep wound,
accepting that I have become a source of pain.
I see now the hurt I've inflicted, the trust eroded,
and I must respect the distance we now face.
Forgive me for the distress I've brought,
for the times when my words weighed heavily.
I took advantage of your compassion,
although not intentionally,
now I must face the repercussions of my actions.
In this new season, I hope for your peace,
unburdened by the weight of my struggles.
In my darkest hours, I mistook your light,
as a beacon to guide me through the night.
Forgive me if I cast you as my saving grace,
it was never yours to heal this fractured mind.
May you find calm and tranquility,
unburdened by all that has passed.

A Fleeting Light

Sunlight touches the morning,
a quiet calm settles in.

Thoughts find their gentle rhythm,
and today feels lighter.

In this simple moment,
recovery whispers softly.

A Promise For Us

In the moments before the day begins,
I hold a promise close,
to care for my heart and mind,
and to give you my best, always.
For you, my dear child, I embrace this journey,
seeking strength and healing with each breath.
Your laughter lights up my world,
a reminder of the love that guides.
When the days feel heavy and the nights too long,
know that my will remains strong.
I am here, working to be whole,
creating a world where joy shines bright
and challenges are met with courage.
I will seek support and find my own path,
to ensure our lives are balanced and full.
I vow to be honest and seek help when needed,
understanding that healing is a daily journey.
Your presence is a gift,
filling my heart with the deepest love.
I commit to being present,
to nurturing both of our spirits with care.
Together, we will find our way,
one step, one day at a time.

A Pillar Of Love

To you, my love,
in my darkest times,
your presence was a steady hand,
a quiet comfort that kept me grounded.
When I felt overwhelmed,
you were my calm,
the gentle pillar that held me up
when everything seemed to be falling apart.
Your eyes, full of care,
were the light I needed
when everything felt so cold.
Your touch eased the pain
that cut deep inside.
In my struggle,
you were the strength I couldn't find alone,
a reminder that healing
comes in small moments,
in the softness of your presence.
Your love is a gift,
offered without condition or end,
guiding me back to hope
when I can't see it myself.

Healing Circles

In circles where our stories transcend,
we find support and hearts to mend,
group therapy's embrace is so true,
where shared voices help us renew.
In every tale and tear released,
we build a bridge to inner peace,
connecting deeply, hearts aligned,
in others' strength, our hope we find.
Together on this path we tread,
healing hearts and hope instead,
in every bond and shared relief,
we find connection in our grief.

Being Seen

In the dim light, my eyes dazed,
a visual flashback sweeps through me,
sharp and vivid, as though I am there again.
Scenes unravel in my mind,
each moment intense, raw
a tide of images crashing in.

The past, once distant,
now breathes heavily at the edge of my awareness,
its presence undeniable,
its impact profound.
I feel the rush, the weight,
the emotional tide pulling me under.

Yet, in the periphery of this storm,
I hold another awareness,
a quiet realization that someone else is here...
my therapist, an unwavering observer
of my external responses to this inner upheaval.
Her presence is a constant safeguard,
an anchor amid the swirling chaos.
I am aware of her gaze,
watchful, compassionate,
tracking the tremors in my body,

the shifts in my breath,
the flicker of my eyes,
the silent dialogue between past and present.

But with this awareness comes another layer,
a web of shame and self-consciousness.
I cringe at the thought of her seeing me
in such a fragile, exposed state,
my defenses crumbling,
control slipping through my fingers.

I am acutely aware of how fragmented I must seem,
a broken mirror reflecting
my most raw and unmasked self,
and it unsettles me to know
that someone is witnessing this unraveling.
The shame of being seen so vulnerable,
so engulfed by my mind, wraps around me,
a cloak of discomfort that only adds
to the turbulence within.

This dual consciousness,
the clash of internal chaos and external observation,
creates a strange juxtaposition of vulnerability and
support.
While the act of being seen is at once
a profound comfort and a source of deep unease,

it also transforms the experience.
What feels like an exposure of my brokenness
becomes a shared journey,
a testament to the strength found
in the delicate balance
of self-discovery and empathetic observation.

Her presence, though daunting,
helps to anchor me through this turbulent sea,
turning isolation into connection,
shame into understanding,
powerlessness into protection,
and the dance between pain and empathy
into a path toward healing.

Day By Day

Waking's a battle, gravity's hold,
the bed's heavy grasp, a comfort so cold.
Air feels like mud, each breath a fight,
morning's a struggle from dawn till night.

Overwhelmed by noise, blinding light's flare,
anxiety tightens, an unending snare.
Routine's a mountain I struggle to climb,
each small task a challenge, a burden in time.

Pretending to be okay is a tireless strain,
a mask I must wear through joy and through pain.
Each smile a disguise, each laugh a thin shell,
I act strong to endure this daily hell.

Yet beside me a heartbeat, soft and true,
a tiny hand reaching, breaking through.
I rise not for me, but for this dear one,
whose needs pull me up with each rising sun.

Each breath, each step, a victory won,
love fuels my strength when the day's begun.
Through overstimulation and ceaseless dread,
I find my way, guided by a smile instead.

Anxiety's Embrace

In the calm of night,
my body whispers distress.
Fatigue drapes heavy on my bones,
heart beats a frantic drum
beneath the skin,
muscles taut as tightropes,
bones trembling, a life of their own.
Dry mouth, a desert
where words crumble to despair,
restless legs beat an anxious rhythm
against sheets that cling too tight.
Indigestion churns, a storm in the gut,
heartburn blazing a trail of fire.
Migraines press a cruel vise,
a relentless pulse against my temples.
Each breath a struggle,
choking down air,
each moment a battle
with the physical echoes of
fear's harsh call.

Whispers Of Light

In the heart of the storm,
where days are measured by the weight of the struggle,
today, a sliver of sunlight breaks through.

The walls still hum with echoes of pain,
but the quiet moments between effort
are like soft breaths of fresh air.

Laughter spills, unexpected,
a melody in the chaos,
and hope, fragile as a new leaf,
dances at the edge of my thoughts.

Here, in the thick of the fight,
a good day blooms, unexpected,
like wildflowers in cracked concrete,
reminding me that even in the depths,
there can be a spark of grace.

Hidden Vault

Inside us, there's this locked-up room,
heavy with old pain, like a secret kept too long.
The key isn't easy to find—
it's buried deep, tangled in our thoughts
and hidden in our feelings.

Unlocking it means diving into the mess,
walking through confusion and fog
where memories jumble together,
and every step feels like trudging through mud.

Emotionally, it's a wild ride,
waves of raw, unfiltered feelings
crashing into the calm we try to maintain,
every burst a reminder of what we'd rather ignore.

Physically, it's a burden we carry,
the tension in our bodies telling stories
of the stress and strain we've kept inside,
reminding us that even our muscles
don't forget the weight of our struggles.

Releasing it all feels like a small rebellion,
a slow shedding of what we've held onto,

finding space for something new,
and letting ourselves breathe again.

It's a journey through our own chaos,
where each step forward is a small victory,
and letting go is just part of the path
toward finding peace and a little bit of freedom.

Hope For Tomorrow

In the slow moments of my day,
there is a subtle promise.

Today may still feel heavy,
but each new moment brings hope
that the weight will ease.

Recovery isn't a straight line,
but a path with curves.
I hold onto the promise
that tomorrow will be kinder,
and with time,
the journey will become easier.

In each step forward,
I find a glimmer of what's possible,
and I know that eventually,
it won't be so hard.

A Field Of Worth

On the field, everything comes alive
in a way that feels both nostalgic and immediate.
The dirt beneath my cleats is warm and welcoming,
its texture grounding me, reminding me that I am here.
The grass carries a scent that is sharp and soothing,
a green, living aroma that fills the air,
mingling with the warmth of the sun
that soaks into my skin,
its heat a gentle reassurance,
a caress that breaks through the cold of doubt.
Before this moment, a sense of dread loomed,
an uncertain fog clouding my thoughts,
leaving me lost, adrift, unsure of where to turn.
But as I move, that haze begins to lift,
replaced by a clear, focused direction.
Around me, the field hums with energy.
The sounds of the game—
the rhythmic thud of a ball in a glove,
the swish of a swing,
the quiet moments between plays—
embrace my pains and aches.
Voices communicate seamlessly,
notes of encouragement, support,
a beautiful exchange that binds us together.

In this newfound clarity, I recognize my strength,
an acknowledgment that I have a place here.
The game becomes a metaphor for my worth,
a counter to the doubts that whisper
I am not enough.
As I play well, validation comes unasked,
a natural reward for my efforts,
not requested, not demanded.
The praise flows not as an obligation,
but as a genuine reflection of my presence.
The passion of each player radiates,
an electric current that pulses through the air,
infusing the game with love and community,
reminding me of the power of connection,
of moving as one under the open sky.
Here, on the field, I feel my own pulse quicken,
a heartbeat that aligns with the rhythm of the game,
and in this dance of movement and sound,
I find a place where joy and purpose converge,
where the simple act of playing
brings me back to myself,
to a feeling of belonging and grace
that I had long forgotten,
and a confidence that I am exactly where I need to be,
validated by the value of my simple existence.

Silently Yearning

In the quiet of the night,
I am tired, deeply exhausted.
The days blend into a blur,
a constant struggle with invisible weights.

I want to feel what it's like
to move through the world effortlessly,
to laugh, to live without the pressure
of relentless thoughts and heavy days.

Each step feels like a climb,
a search for some semblance of normalcy,
and though the path is long and winding,
I yearn for moments of ease.

Embracing The Journey

As dawn's first light breaks the night's embrace,
I stand anew with resolve in place.
The scars from the battles, though deeply ingrained,
mark the journey of strength I've attained.

Each fight with the storm, each clash with despair,
teaches me courage and how to repair.
I've learned to embrace both the pain and the plight,
for each battle fought is a step toward the light.

The path ahead may twist and bend,
with new challenges that will test and transcend.
Yet I've gathered my tools and I know how to steer,
through the darkness and doubts, my path will be clear.

If new challenges come, I'll know how to ask,
in seeking help, I'll uncover what's masked.
Support is a compass when paths are unclear,
guiding me gently through every new fear.

So here's to the battles and hurdles I face,
to the strength and the wisdom I gain in this place.
With each step I take and each breath I renew,
I meet the unknown with a spirit that's true.

To those who've stood by me, both near and afar,
professionals and loved ones, each a guiding star,
I thank you for your wisdom, your patience, your care,
your unwavering support, and the love that you share.

And to myself, I offer a grateful embrace,
for choosing to fight and not falter in grace.
With each step I've taken and every fight I've braved,
I am proud of my strength and the progress I've made.